For Every Kind Of Ache

J. Aradhana

BookLeaf Publishing

India | USA | UK

Made with ❤ on the BookLeaf Publishing Platform

www.bookleafpub.in

www.bookleafpub.com

Dedication

To the ones that need a hand around their shoulder

But do not have one.

It's Alright. Have Faith in You.

You Are Enough.

Acknowledgement

I would like to deeply acknowledge, honour and pay respect to the few, unexpected, very valuable and cherish worthy moments, that bettered my dark days—here and there and now and then.

Each singular moment started a series of both belief and life-altering situations.

Recalling them feels like looking at tiny specks of faraway stars in a pitch-black sky,

Taking turns to brighten up, without being asked to. Today, if I am dejected about something,

Those rare moments are a big reminder to simply 'Hang on'.

Preface

Many years ago when I was studying in school, we had the daily duty of wiping clean the classroom's blackboard and writing a quote on the upper edge of the board. One fine morning as I was stepping off the chair after having done so, a fellow student who had been watching in silence, asked in a concerned tone, 'Why do you always write such serious quotes?' I turned around to see what I had just written. The quote read: *'Life is not a bed of roses.'* What is wrong with that, I wondered. It felt true to me. Yet it seemed to have upset her. I wiped it off the very next morning and thereafter quit putting up quotes. I did not want to upset any more of the students. At the same time, the situation made me question myself if, in-fact something was wrong with me. (I was in the 7th grade and 12 years of age at the time.)

The reason I mention this incident here, is to reassure that each of us is 'wired' differently. There can be numerous reasons as to 'why' each of us is a certain way but the more important question is: How accepting are we of ourselves? It took me another two decades to come to terms with my own understanding of the world, what I seemed to relate to, who I found comfort in, what I liked reading, talking about, and writing.

Sensitive, overly sensitive, and emotional are some of the terms I have been labeled with and have grown accustomed to hearing. Nevertheless, I carry on writing how I am able to, about everything in life that has influenced me. Be it people, the various circumstances that have left a mark or even the magnificent nature that impacts us profoundly—if only we pay attention to it.

For Every Kind of Ache is a poetry book with words written *from* every kind of ache. This book is indeed the result of a writing challenge with BookLeaf Publishing and I am thankful for the opportunity. The bigger challenge for me, however, has been to consciously bare my mind for the first time and put my words and my unfiltered understanding of the world out there, for you to read and hopefully read again.

1. Life: An Amalgamation of Moments.

(i)

I found myself under a stillborn sky

That was seething over

A slow-brewing tide; which in turn looked
furious

In the absence of the moon overhead. I sigh,

At the quite obvious discord

Between three majestic faces of nature

Whilst aimlessly throwing pebbles

Into the water around.

Every pebble when dropped

Created a ripple

On the surface pretty and then

Proceeded to slowly drown.

(ii)

Drop, a drop of dew I had spotted

At the crack of dawn

Looked like a teardrop

Sitting on the blade of a young grass

It reminded me of the teardrop coming from
the eye

Of dear old Rocky, our gentle lab

When he is cathartically overjoyed

Or when he sees our suitcases in the Foyer.

'Don't go,' he tried to say

But could never make it sound.

He is no more now.

Don't go, we felt aloud

Towards the end of his time but to no avail.
Thus,

Tears shed in such torn moments tug hard at
a heart

That has learnt to cope in silence from every
kind of loss

That had been compounding all along.

(iii)

Tug, as in a tugboat that tows

Big broken-down ships back to port.

So, they can be fixed in order to resume

Many a voyage again.

The amount of pain I felt, from having lost

My dad—the Captain to death had me wishing

My spirit be towed away from a body ageing weary

With remorse.   Towed away

From under the unhelpful pre-mature sky

I was seeking refuge in. Meanwhile, the sky was

All but waiting to spill over its rage, like me,

At the plight it unexpectedly found itself in.

We both seemed to share a similar uneasy
void

We did not know how, to get rid of.

(iv)

Life, is an amalgamation of moments, I realize

As I walk in search of waters

To drown and leave behind every devastating
memory.

A tiny grain under the vastness, I seemed to
be

Standing vulnerable in front of the wide
universe whereas

The universe did not shy away

From making bare *its own helplessness.*

I was a tiny grain in the universe one moment

And then it dawned upon me that

I am the Universe.

I am my own storm. I am my own sunshine.

I am my own thunder and I am my own

Calm in the skies.

I am Life and I am learning to live,

Hoping to love and most of all trying

To overcome every kind of trial to simply
Survive.

2. Home is where the Hope is.

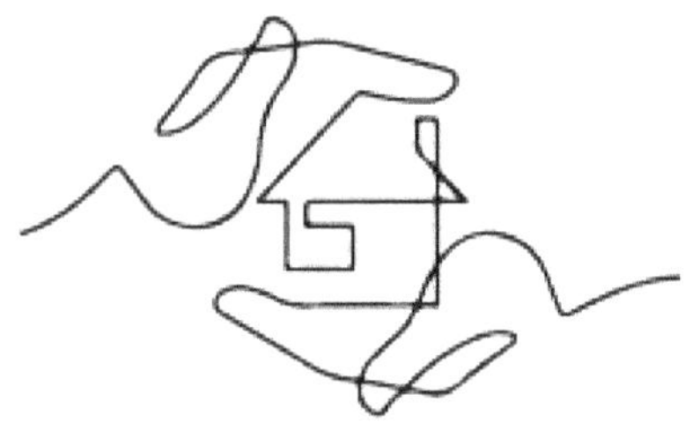

Where are the caring bonds

Where is the innocent laughter

Where are the alerting cries

Of various high-flying raptors.

Where is the sound of rain

On that beautiful terrain

Where is the gust of wind

With no trace of dust on its face.

Where are the kindest of spirits

Or the sound of their silent prayers.

Where are the loud-tolling bells

That remind us of divine powers.

Where is the burning desire

Of re-living yesteryears precious

Where is the steady hope

That the next year will be even better.

'Home is where the heart is'

Is all we ever hear.

Why does it not occur to us

That Home is where good hope is.

Home is where the Hope is.

3. The Lemon Tree.

'If only trees can tell us aloud that our end is near.'

Standing tall in the cemented backyard

Of my maternal house, grows,

A lemon tree wild without being cared for as much these days.

From up the terrace the length of its branches

One can see spread out and over

The neighbour's house adjacent

Bearing green and yellow lemons.

The first time I picked a freshly dropped
lemon

I could not believe the size or smell of it.

And as I tasted it, my eyes widened with
delight.

Lemons can taste this good? I quipped. Mother
smiled.

The house smelled lemony and wonderfully
so,

Right from outside its gated doors.

The Pickle, came soon after and for one whole
summer

That's all I had my rice with. Until one fine
day

She conveyed, in a sad tone:

'The Tree, was in full bloom for quite some
time that year

No other summer had we seen it that way.

It kept dropping what felt like hundreds of
lemons

That he was so very thrilled at the sight of it.

He had to call the grocers to take them away

Just so they didn't all go waste.

And by the end of that summer your father
was gone.'

I stand below the tree now, on my every visit
home

Watching my daughter attempt to pluck

The few scattered lemons down

With a long hooked stick mother made.

Did it happen again? I ask her as she watches.

No, she replied. And never before either.

It was the one time that year until right
before he left.

Do trees know? I wonder, touching the old
hard bark

About when it was time for the soul that
cared for them to leave?

15

Because the Lemon tree Father planted seems
to have bid

A most grateful goodbye long before we did.

4. God was Once a Little Girl.

The luscious liquid silver looked like

It was adorned with many a shiny sparkle

That, beneath the morning sun, lit up as it flowed.

It felt as though, a little girl had sprinkled with glee

All her favorite glitter across the wide river.

The seamless waters then rushed to pour along

Slippery mountain slides in a mighty careless manner.

Their sprays were a fleeting sideways rain.

She clap, clapped her hands with a bountiful joy

As she caught hold of many an abiding spray.

Come nightfall and deep from under the layers

Of a sound asleep water, the moon she scoops out

To hold and adore in the palms

Of her gentle and warm hands.

And at sunrise, to a sweet melodic voice

She ecstatically responds, long before
knowing

It was a cuckoo singing. Meanwhile,

The cuckoo sang on, not knowing

It was a child serenading.

Either God had a little girl and made the
world for her

Because He believed she would make the
most of it.

Or better yet, God was once a little girl.

For how else would He have known

What filled her soul with joy to the brim.

5. Goldmine Goodbyes.

Hurt a little, it does

When whoever bids goodbye walks away

Not having once turned back.

Do they not want to know

If we were still waiting

Standing *still* as we watch them go.

Every goodbye is a goldmine of a moment

Frozen in time, emotion and circumstance.

So much so, that many a time

We remember them more

Than the moments we first met and said
hello.

Some of us, therefore wait until

The image of that friend or the lover

Or the foe or the kind stranger

Has faded out of our sight—a sight that lives

Etched in our minds forever.

6. It started with Adam.

When kindness spoke, it sounded

Like sweet honey dew drops.

She couldn't help but pick

From within the shrouding wind. Well,

How can anyone fathom sweetness

To be ill-willed. And so,

He slithered away that night

Having fed her with courage enough. While
she, thereafter

Came to be drawn forever

As the original sinner

Having handed over the apple

To her sleeping beloved

Who rose and ignorantly ate of it.

A man's innocence was thus born

Having blamed a woman for the first time.

What could she do but remain in silence;

In the midst of two or three against one.

Don't we even now?

7. Rivers do Cry first before they Flood.

Tears well up within the walls of her eyes

Akin to a river swelling up whilst trying hard to contain

Its waters within the man-made banks.

For it knows what it is capable of

If it chose to flow free and fast.

And when eventually a time had come, alas,

When it felt overwhelmed and couldn't help

The overbearing; it let loose itself

Tearing up, every floodgate on its path

So much so,

The world around could now see

The liberation, it was capable of giving itself.

Time and again, it serves mankind as a great big reminder

That its existence was never meant to be contained.

For no walls were too high.

No city too wide.

No miles it couldn't breach.

No sea it couldn't reach.

Why ask a woman what you cannot ask a river?

We were never made to be contained.

Were we?

8. Profound Truths.

How do we know

To wait for the rain to pour

When the soil from afar starts to smell alive

We call it *petrichor.*

How do we know

To spot the tiny dew drops

Sitting pretty on green grass

Right after the morning mist fades

Having bathed the green clean.

How do we know

To find solace by watching

The moon in the distance

In clueless times.

How did we know

We would find peace in its calm.

How do we know

That the stars weren't already

Watching over us

As we fix our eyes on their twinkle

At the end of a dull, void day.

How do we know

To run to the Gods

When we're breaking apart and have

Nowhere else to go.

Why do we believe

They live up in heaven

And not amongst us.

How do we know this certain truth?

Why do we only

Thank the angel that saves

But never the conniving devil

That very often shows

Its true-blue colors.

Why is it so

The infant cries aloud first

When out of the womb.

How did it know

It's out of its only safe haven.

If we put together one and one

And two and two.

A child may know the answer. Well,

Why can't the world come together

Just like them numbers do.

Why don't we remind ourselves

That the rainbow we so admire

Looks amazing only because

It shows its colors all at once.

Would we be as amused

If it showed them one at a time.

How did we learn

To live for each ourselves

Where is the unity? Why aren't we,

Like rainbow colors.

9. Unheard Of.

Listen I,

I thus spake

And yet again you were gone

Before the lashes could lift themselves

Aye, so the eyes could eye you well.

The wind never can settle down

You once told me. I agree, but

35

The wind

Has no body.

10. None left to dance with.

Fumes fill the woods I take shelter in

The night sky wore

A smoked solitude. As did I.

It seemed to have danced tirelessly

With every kind of star that shone bright and not

With a desire to find love.

But doesn't love almost always prove to be

Deaf and mute. Some of us have

Weak hearts that yearn constant

To keep brimming with the light

Burning bright like the Cosmos.

How do you rest it?

How do you un-feel it?

How do you not fulfill it?

How do you stop yourself

From polluting your own soul again?

We were done dancing now

There seemed to be none left

To dance with. Not that I care anymore.

For I was done dancing

There just seems to be none

That can mend or make me feel whole.

What is   Whole?

11. The Fall.

Snowflakes, slow falling on the skin of my face

I look up wanting to feel more of them

They slow fall on the palm of my hand, I extend

To receive them

As they Fall with grace.

Raindrops, wore the sound of a rapid fall

I look down and away from; the cold blunt
arrow shots.

Proprioceptors alert, I run to take cover from.

From being drenched as they hit the ground.

Is this how we fall too?

Whilst falling,

We either drown the ones around us in our
raining mess

As we disappear — to be lost in our
woundedness *Or*

Do we sink gradual in a sorrow

That is slow in punishing

Just like the severe winter weather.

May we understand that — how we Fall

Actually matters. Not just to us

But to the ones around us as well.

12. Motherhood is what Motherhood does.

That first time you saw me

A broad smile and wisps of hair over my stone face.

A long oiled mane, had I.

Braided as though

I've been in existence

Since quite a few centuries ago

'*You're such an old soul,*' you told me. I frowned.

Isn't that how you knew me? Hands folded.

A perfect portrait of a picture. Black and
white

Standing tall. I looked like royal gold.

You knew me young

You knew me dynamic

You knew me bold

You called me fearless.

Now me, well, I carry

Sweet babe in my arms and I live surprisingly,

With an excess of caution and care.

Two words that meant nothing before

Because of sweet babe by my side

The bold and fearless I willingly lose

As I watch her grow

Reigning in my rage.

Motherhood is beautiful yet

Motherhood is smothering most times.

Motherhood I guess, is what motherhood
does to you

And I am amused at the power an infant has

To unwittingly be able to change a grown
adult.

45

13. She grew a wall up her Heart.

The moorlands were home, having arrived

In the heart of a barren wild, she lived

Unafraid of the dark; undeterred by
masculine lies.

The moorlands felt home. Therein she shone

Like an unforgiving moon, no star

Would dare side with. And when on the edge

She refused to let sink deep

47

Desire, sailing fast in her veins. The sight

Of slithering, smooth bodies often found

Lying bare in the sands; at times entwined

For long past sunrise reminded her

Of the wicked, undying vines growing slow
and living entangled

Within the walls of a lacklustre house.

The world she had built in her mind

To keep herself from being dejected

Had built a sturdy wall

Up her own heart. She couldn't

Tear it down. Hence, turned into

A mare fleeing far until it felt liberated.

The moorland was her home; her heart,

A fortress she has vowed to be the only
Queen of.

14. For Vizag.

Fifteen summers later

On the plane to Vizag, I regain the voice

That had long disappeared yet

Knew to come alive when my feet touched the
ground — I still call home.

It said to me, 'I have images of a younger you

I have been unable to erase.'

I don't say a word. Meanwhile, I find

Its streets had well preserved the same old innocent quiet

That made me want to stay and never leave again.

If only, they had been

Chaotic as hell, I would have fled

With a fine excuse

From whatever heaven this was

Flowing effortless all around. For I seem

To have never forgotten

Pictures of a compassionate people

Lodged in my mind deep.

Oh, how deep of a well the mind can be.

It is truly baffling. Nevertheless,

I coyishly tell the very delightful sea's breeze

'I don't know if you know, but

I've come back to breathe your very air

I once grew up breathing in.'

15. The Value of Patience.

A seed buried in the ground

Knows it will sprout

As it waits for a soggy cloud to float over

And be ready to pour. The water

Spreads all over the ground

Rooting the little life in firmness

They said, 'Wait for it.

The wait is always worth it.'

She was a seed waiting to sprout

As she eyed a soggy cloud waiting to pour
over

And drench her soul. It turned out to be

An unending fall that left her

Cold to the bone thus, awakening

From within her — a frail tune

a tiny piece of music

a melody

a longing song — that gave consolation.

It was one that grew in strength gradual

To eventually branch out

And hold captive in its story

Every bird that came by

So, they could nestle and breed

With a never-before assurance. The birdlings

Born unaware, sing free and loud

What their mothers could only hum

They sing aloud, what their mothers could
only utter

In hush prayers.

'Be patient,' they said. 'The wait is always
worth it. The wait,

Is always worth it.' I do ask myself at times

For how many generations have our women
dreamt

To be able to breathe free and soar easy.
Because of them

Now some of us finally do.

16. The Woodpecker.

Stance unfaltering, he chips away

At the rust of a robust heart.

Frigid was the sight

Of an unblinking viciousness

As the nail-like beak sounded louder

With every strong peck.

The cells in my brain drown

Pained to the sound, so much so, that

Many a past pain living in the conscious

Felt oblivious.

I grew my hope every morn' to see

This unwarily frequent lover appear

At my window sill again.

If only I could hold you, thought I

From my side of the infrangible glass

As he gazed intent. If only,

I could hold you. Would you,

Trust me enough to remain calm

Or would you flutter and fly away

Like all the insecure

That came before you did.

17. About the Caged bird.

I never had a fair chance at life, I tell my beloved.

And the older I age I feel it is so unfair, I say.

He is a wonderful man and often times I wonder

If it is because he is wonderful — that I finally feel safe

To speak the unspeakable.

There are millions of young girls around the
world

Groomed to perfection. Raised,

To breed in submission. A caged life.

'I know why the caged bird sings,' Maya
Angelou wrote.

I cannot agree more.

Meanwhile, I know why many a caged bird

Don't sing too.

They just never found their voice. *Worse,*

Some don't recognize it anymore. Even worse,

Maybe they tried too hard to be heard and
alas,

Gave up, having lost the one good thing

Nobody should ever lose and that is Hope.

18. Hope, my dear.

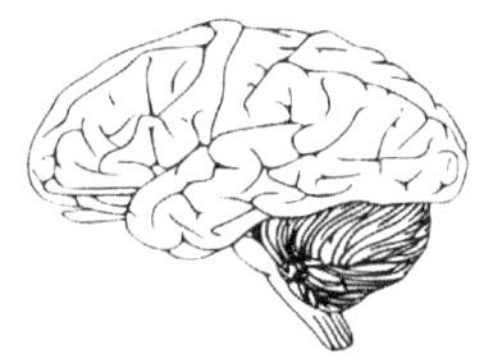

Hope, doesn't fall from the sky.

Hope, is not the bright morning sunrise

Flooding the room after a most horrid night.

Well, disagree all you want but

I never heard the sun say so, did you?

Also, does it mean that the people living in places,

Where the sun doesn't rise for many a month,

Live hopeless? I rest my case.

We see hope because we want to see it.

We feel hopeful because we've made

A mighty effort - to feel so.

We look for hope in all things around

Because we need someone or something
telling us

That 'everything is going to be okay.'

In truth, we want to hear from elsewhere

When we cannot find the strength to tell
ourselves

That 'everything is indeed going to be alright'

In order to make it through, another day.

One day at a time. One moment at a time.

Hope helps us preserve our innate selves in
some way.

It helps preserve our sanity, in order to keep
living

And to be able to lift ourselves up

When the world won't. Well, why should it?

And how many at a time, can it?

We remember to remain hopeful

Because it is our last resort — to not give up.

Even when people and circumstances tell us
otherwise.

Hope, I have learnt my dear

Is the flame in our brain fixated at finding

The bright side of dark.

It is the little feel of a voice inside of us,
disallowing us

From letting ourselves down. Especially,

When life feels so very fragile

And the world in all its glory, turns its back
on us.

That is hope, in all its truth.

The ever-persisting fight from within.

The will to wake and let life have another try.

19. Hold me.

Hold me

While you cry.

I've built my steely shoulders stronger

For you to put your head on.

When you are ridden with misery, weep it out

Go on and drench me, if it helps

Unburden the angst. Just let it down on me.

Scream at me, if it makes the furiousness

Less intense. I am willing to hear it out.

Just don't do it all alone. Well, I have always

Only done it all alone. And the pain

Of not having another soul present added

To the volatility of a depthless despair even
more.

Hold me. Don't cry no more.

No eye deserves to cry.

No soul deserves to cry.

Each of us needs to know

That we are so much more than the tears

That fall from our tired eyes.

Hold me. Don't cry no more.

No eye deserves to cry.

20. One with the Trees.

Speak to me as you always do and

With your most nimble touch, may your leaves

Caress the skin on my face as I,

Close my eyes wishing to remain in peace

In the faintest of your fragrant smell.

Because I can smell well

The smell of your roots

Your astounding truth

Your magnificent growth that has been
happening

Since ages before my own birth.

Your ever glorious sight makes me wish

I was somehow one with you. Or at the least

One among you. Oh, how I imagine —

We would breeze the world together. And

In the vastness of our sturdy, long branches

Shelter the birds and their babes.

Come eve, I see us lay back and

Watch the skies go slowly home.

Bathe we would in the flirtatious rains

And stand strong in the storms to come.

But why does it storm, I wonder? Did we
make

The skies upset? Like a man does his wife

For no good reason.

Our pretty leaves, we watch them play

With the mischievous and gutsy gale

As it rushes to God knows where.

And in the face of a scorching sun, we stand
tall

With our chests out, feeling proud about
providing our shade

Unbiased to one and all

I wish I was one with the trees, I often think
to myself.

I just wish I was one with them.

Trees have never hurt me. They have only
given me

A lot more than I can ask for.

21. Summer

Refused to stay. Came in

A cold frost numbing. It owned.

I write two million things

About those warm and giving eyes

But do not a word say.

I am the Summer. I am never asked

To stay. So, I give way to the cold frost

It comes hugging like a wounded bear

In search of a resting place

To lay down, its presence weighed.

 I watch her write two million things

About how life thrives under my stead and
Yet,

She has never, a word of gratitude said.

I am the Summer. I was never asked to stay.

www.ingramcontent.com/pod-product-compliance
Lightning Source LLC
LaVergne TN
LVHW041225200726

843507LV00013B/2581